CONTENT

WHAT IS

POSSIBLE ?

What is possible? In the subject of a person's life I know it is greater than anything we could dare to dream or imagine. With every new life that comes into the world, comes a beautiful opportunity, a fresh start – the possibility of a life lived in love and joy– and the opportunity to be a world-changer. As parents or kids' pastors, it's such a privilege and opportunity to be a significant part of this. The weight of that opportunity echoes through Proverbs 22:6: 'Start children off on the way they should go, and even when they are old they will not turn from it.' (Message Bible)

I understand the principle, but when I come to what to do practically, that's where I wish this Proverb were a little longer than 21 words. For me it leaves a great question unanswered – What does it look like look like to start a child off in the right way?

In this book, I track my own search for how we create kids of Jesus, not just kids of our earthly family or of church, but kids of Jesus. He says that we are his in the Bible, right? So it must be possible to raise kids of Jesus. Just imagine the possibilities – how that would change the face of Christianity, the church, wider society, and ultimately, the world. Imagine what would be possible with children all over the world growing up and becoming just like Jesus.

HIS KIDS, HIS KINGDOM

In Luke 18:15 (NIV), Jesus says: 'Let the little children come to me, and do not hinder them, for the kingdom of God belongs to such as these. Truly I tell you, anyone who will not receive the kingdom of God like a little child will never enter it.' What sticks out to me in this verse is 'like a little child' – it is provocative, clear language showing that this process isn't mystical or just 'spiritual', but the ability is already inside us in the way God created and formed us as children. It also spoke to me of a link between the process of how a child develops and the process of how the Kingdom develops in our lives.

I know that part of the context of this scripture is Jesus referring to spiritual rebirth, but I also believe the same process parallels our physical birth. Either way, Jesus is pointing us towards a process – a physiological, psychological and spiritual process that works together to form his kingdom in us.

My passion and hope is that we can draw on that parallel from day one in raising our kids into the fullness of his Kingdom – for children to be raised into a Kingdom which is not just about 'getting to heaven', but about building a kingdom in which God is the ruler of all we do in our lives here on earth, a kingdom not defined by membership or material treasures, but by the hearts and actions of its people who are just like their king, Jesus. Like Jesus taught us to pray: 'Your Kingdom come, your will be done, on earth as in heaven.'

I pray that this book blesses you and gives you a fresh perspective and understanding of how to build with generations. I also pray that if you are a pastor or parent, this book will give you fresh hope, energy and wisdom to build the church or family you've always dreamed of.

ASKING

BIG

QUESTIONS

I'm a fairly regular Christian guy, brought up in the church and always involved in one way or another. One of the areas I'd served in while I was growing up in my late teens and during my early 20s was the children's work, which I'd served in for around five years. Eventually, I guess I would say I grew out of it and wanted to work with adults. I kind of had a viewpoint that serving in kids' ministry was a stage of life to progress from, and that it should be left to people who feel called to be kids' workers, right?

Fast-forward about 8 years, specifically to about 3 years ago, the start of the whole journey I've written about. At that time, I was a commercial project manager working for a normal, regular, non-Christian business and quite happy with it as well. However, I was still very passionate about church, so when I was approached by the church to come and work for them in the business department, I gladly took the step, ignorant of my forthcoming fate.

You know how sometimes the word 'yes' can be dangerous in church? Well I said it and I managed to find myself in charge of our children's ministry – I'm not sure how, but I think it was down to that 'yes' word. I have to confess it wasn't my first choice and I was really reluctant, as I didn't see it as a particularly important area of church life. I was short sighted. But there was just something about it. I felt it was the right thing to do. I know we can never be certain, but it felt as if God was asking, and I didn't want to get that wrong, so I agreed. Very quickly, I stepped into looking after over 200 kids every Sunday, unsure, but with a determination to do my best for God.

I have been genuinely amazed, challenged to the core, totally heartbroken and inspired by what I discovered.

I have to share what some of our kids are going through and why we have to wake up to the reality of their lives. Let's take the story of a seven-year-old child in our church, just an average kid from a good Christian family who come every week to church, regularly worship, pray, know the Bible, but one week, they were just not themselves. I took time out from what I was 'supposed to be doing' as I knew they needed to talk. So we sat there as the child told me about how their dad had walked out on them. He had told them to choose who they loved – mum or dad – and that if they chose their mum, they wouldn't be seeing him again

Our kids are dealing with adult issues at the ages of 6, 7, 8, 9, 10, that are raising in them huge questions about God, Christians and church, issues which are potentially destroying their faith and even their futures long-term. I was certain that our 'cool' kids' church, great as it was, just wasn't scratching where it was itching for this kid, and if that was the case, how many other kids were also unfulfilled in their relationship with God and their experience of his Kingdom?

"I QUESTIONED MYSELF:
HOW ARE WE
RAISING OUR KIDS
AND DOES IT WORK?"

I questioned myself: How are we raising our kids and does it work?

It led me on a search to discover how to build generationally. This isn't something we should leave to chance; this is something I would advise that you seriously prioritise. Whatever you sow now in your spiritual training of kids, you will reap in years to come. Are you comfortable with how you are doing that?

The whole process of generational growth is much more subtle than we think and its impact is huge. Let me take the church generation of my childhood, for example – we were all raised in a good kids' church, where church was an environment for us to meet our friends, have some fun, have a drink and a snack, be taught the Bible and go home. Does this sound familiar in any way? Does my generation today come to church to meet friends, grab a drink at the church coffee shop, listen to the Word and head off? It's hardly the dynamic life-changing church we dream of, but it's what we were trained to do as children. It's deep in our subconscious values and beliefs that church is for us – that we come and receive and we have to be taught the latest things of God by our leaders, and that that's the best or only way to hear God. Subconsciously, we were taught that church is a Sunday thing, an occasion for 'my friends and me'. It is very subtle and not overtly destructive, but it is an extremely effective way of keeping churches contained, small and introspective. The process is subtle because children learn this behaviour not from what we teach from the platform, but how we model it in the way we 'do' church – the weekly practices, which first become habits and eventually, values.

Now, I'm not disrespecting the hard work that went into our kids ministry growing up; it's given me a great foundation, so these things aren't all 'bad' as long as they are balanced out with what Jesus actually called us to do: love the world, include them, make disciples, reach the lost, bring the kingdom of heaven to earth. But this is where we are often lost ourselves. We were never trained to do this at a younger age.

There are no subconscious pathways for our minds to freely and naturally do this, as we never experienced it at a young enough age for it to be in our core values or belief systems. It is often removed from what our children's churches train us to do. So it's often overlooked in our lives, or it's a real effort, a struggle, an unnatural, even weird thing we try to do. So, rather than Christians just naturally doing these things and building amazing welcoming, life-changing, organic God-filled communities, because these values were not built into our core values and beliefs as children, we've had to compensate. In our generation, our solution is for our churches to become professional, with professional Sunday services and events and professional outreach ministries, because we don't know how to do it naturally as part of who we are. That's because we don't, in our core values and beliefs, have any pathways built in to do any of the above. We never had the idea invested in us that we can do it as an individual, without a professional or ministry framework to support us.

REAL FAITH IN A REAL WORLD

More than ever, our children need a real faith, because the reality of a fallen world is all too often their personal reality. Society has changed; it wasn't waiting for us and it shows no sign of slowing down for us to catch up. My passion is that we stay at the forefront of society, ensuring that our faith is relevant and robust in the society in which our kids live. We have to put genuine effort and energy into this, as the rate of change is quicker than ever before, especially in the last decade. Huge leaps forward in technology and communication have served to rapidly accelerate this process. These two developments have opened up the floodgates of information, both good and bad, and made them accessible to the masses, dramatically affecting childhood.

The access to televisions, mobile phones, tablets and computers is staggering, and most children are now growing up without the boundaries, filters and censorship we had to protect us in previous generations. The world is also now more open than ever. There are less and less 'behind closed door' issues that kids don't know about, be it through technology or the openness of parents trying to cope with these social changes. As a result, society has had to adapt, and the knock-on effect is that childhood is dying a rapid death. The BBC recently reported that in a survey taken on an online forum for mothers, the most common view – from more than two thirds of the group – was that childhood now ended at age 12. A third of respondents to the poll thought childhood was over even sooner – by the age of 10.[1]

The signs are unfortunately out there for all to see. One example would be the issue of the sexualisation of children. Take for example one of the current issues, 'sexting'. In a 2012 research report, the NSPCC found that 'The primary technology-related threat comes from peers, not stranger danger.'[2] Between the ages of 13-14 in particular, this is becoming a peer-to-peer social issue that our children have to deal with as part of their society. This demonstrates a huge shift in the issues they face, and subsequently, we need to keep up with and continually review and revise our educational approach. Let's take another example from the 2011 Bailey review 'Letting Children Be Children: Report of an independent review of the commercialisation and sexualisation of childhood.' The report cited the pressure children are now coming under from a range of sources to act as consumers. Companies are targeting our children earlier and younger to get them to become consumers, which unless handled correctly, has the potential to instil unhelpful and destructive values and beliefs in our children.[3] Yet another example is a recent poll by the Association of Teachers and Lecturers, which in a 2013 study, indicated that children aged 10 years old talk about dieting and being skinny. Even more shockingly, children as young as 4 years old were refusing to eat certain foods for fear of becoming fat.

Spend enough time around children in a safe, honest environment and you won't even need a report to see that these issues, and many others, are having an effect on our children's future. There is a common and rapidly increasing trend that these issues are becoming important at earlier and earlier ages.

There's an English phrase 'The early bird catches the worm', and when it comes to a child's development, this is so true. Early influences in a child's life are key. The shocking truth is that research suggests that by the age of ten, most of our values, which create our beliefs, are formed.

Your core values and beliefs are the formation of the deepest and hardest-to-reach parts of the brain, the subconscious. The influences children face, and our responses to them in this period, will have a significant underlying effect on their lives for years to come, as our responses contribute to their values and beliefs. And as this development is deeply subconscious – not constructed through conscious thought – children (and often us as parents and leaders) are completely unaware of the development, never realising it is taking place. If you fast forward from this period, say 10 years to your early 20s, and you are at the place where you try to change the values and beliefs that have developed because at that point you become aware that you no longer want to live by them (if that even ever happens), then it takes time, sometimes a lot of time (ten years in my personal experience), and I don't know about you but I would rather save our kids from that.

Adulthood has already arrived for many of our kids, and as a church, I feel we are under prepared for it. Do we really know how to demonstrate real faith in a real world?

[1]   **Modern childhood 'ends at age of 12'. BBC News.**
       Available at: http://www.bbc.co.uk/news/education-21670962
       (Accessed on 9th May 2013)
[2]   **A qualitative study of children, young people and 'sexting'. NSPCC.**
       Available at: http://www.nspcc.org.uk/informresourcesforprofessionals/sexualabuse/sexting-research_wda89260.html
       (Accessed on 9th May 2013)
[3]   *Bailey, R (2011) Report of an Independent Review of the Commercialisation and Sexualisation of Childhood Department for Education.*
       Available at: https://www.gov.uk/government/uploads/system/uploads/attachment_data/file/175418/Bailey_Review.pdf
       (Accessed on: 9th May 2013)

"RESEARCH SUGGESTS THAT BY THE AGE OF TEN, MOST OF OUR VALUES, WHICH CREATE OUR BELIEFS, ARE FORMED."

LONG-TERM VISION

Without a specific vision to do so, is it even possible to raise up Kids of Jesus?

The Bible says: 'Without vision, people perish.' This is something I've been aware of in church, especially in the UK, that there has been this never-ending 'battle' of younger generations leaving churches. This is not a new issue, but my passion is that we never let the question of why they leave become old.

The reasons younger generations leave church change all the time, and I understand that when boiled down to the core, these choices are personal decisions that each individual has to make them for themselves. But my question is – As a church or a family, how easily do we help them to navigate their choices? And more than that: are we even aware of a choice being made before it's too late?

Having been brought up in church, I was aware that 'younger' generations would leave the church. When I was younger, the ministry to young people was all about getting solid foundations in so that when 'they' went to university, 'they' would be okay. As I got older, it was all about the 'youth' – making youth work great – as the youth were not engaging in church and it was hard to get our teenagers to come to church.

However, as society changes, so does the age at which young people make this choice as they grow up – the point at which they 'come of age'. My passion is that with this generation, we don't get caught out or forced onto the back foot, but that we have a robust vision and plan to facilitate their coming of age.

I think that as Christians, our awareness of the pace at which society and culture changes helps or hinders us hugely in this issue. I would ask you to take an honest (but not condemning) look and ask the question: Are we paying today for the values and beliefs we put into our children ten years' ago?

I would like you to question how you build God's family or your children's church. How does a child's experience of what you model of God shape their values and beliefs about Christianity and church? What beliefs and values would a child hold from the example of your children's church by the time they're 10 years old? I'm not just asking about what you teach them, but the whole process of your development of them Is it full of grace and acceptance, love and truth? How do you discipline your kids? How do you shape them? What do you expect of them? How do they outwork their faith? How do they use their spiritual gifts? How do they advance God's kingdom? How do they engage with others? Most importantly, how do they cultivate their own relationship with God?

The reason I ask this question is a checkpoint to make sure you are not inadvertently building something that you're going to spend the next ten years having to fight against, knock down and rebuild.

Are you waiting until your children are mature, maybe 15 or 16, or even over 18 or in their early 20s – whatever the age we put on it – that point when they have 'come of age' before you give them the real deal of what Christianity is about? God has no grandchildren, only children. We don't need to dumb God down for children, or make our teaching of him purely intellectual. When we do that, we are in danger of putting upcoming generations through all the pain and hardship of thinking they had it all okay, only to find out they were wrong. That's what I think we've been doing through our own ignorance for generations. We are raised one way with a set experience of church, then when we have 'come of age', we are expected to flip our faith around and totally live in a way that challenges our core beliefs and values that were set in the same church.

Let me explain what I mean. We teach our kids in a nice way, in nice Sunday schools, and they do everything we ask of them. They sit and we teach – it's all based on our initiative as leaders – the kids just have to turn up and church is all about them. They sit, they listen, we lead, we tell them about God. Then suddenly, as they 'come of age', they have to completely flip their core beliefs and values about how they should live as a Christian. They find out that even though they have diligently followed how we 'do church', all of a sudden the way they internalised the Christian life as a child is wrong; it's all about what real Christians do when they have 'come of age'. In this stage, there is a huge value and belief shift, where for example they are expected to give to the church, to find God for themselves in a 'quiet time' and many other expectations to be self-sufficient, to contribute and to live a life that reflects Jesus, when most of these fundamental are often almost polar opposite to what we have taught them as children, especially through environment of our Sunday. This can easily cause battles between leaders and their youth congregations as they 'come of age'. It's because they do everything that we ask of them, but then we move the goal posts as to how they should be and what the 'right' way to live as a Christian is. The same people who teach them one set of values and beliefs then reject them for different values and beliefs, causing pain and confusion in the process.

To give an example, let's take the subject of church being for 'us' or for 'reaching the lost'. On the whole, most churches work hard to make children's church a place our kids (ages 0-10) love to come to. We do things they love and want to do. We teach our kids the Bible and its meaning on a Sunday morning, sing nice songs to God and worship him. Maybe we have group time and talk about how God can help them. We give the kids a drink and a snack and make church very comfortable. We're all on the same page, in the same place with God, and church is very much a great place for us.

However once the children have 'come of age', let's say in their early to mid-twenties, we now 'expect' these adults to reach out, invite, and bring people to church. We teach that Church is not just about them, but about others, and we now want them to invite unsafe people into the church and it's not going to be comfortable. If those same people have grown up in the church, this can confuse and alienate 'good' people who have gone with the flow, but who now have to change their core values and beliefs. This is a long and often painful process and one that we, or they, often struggle to get our or their heads around. This is of course assuming there is an absence of a smooth transition or a healthy robust strategy for when they 'come of age'. Without this, the dramatic shift in values often pushes them to one of two options: painful personal change, or leaving church. Without the maturity that comes at different ages for different young adults, generations often end up confused, hurt, and feeling rejected, like there's something wrong with them, that there's nothing here for them, that they don't fit in, that the church doesn't love them. Sound familiar?

Now I realise the subject of church either being for 'us', or for 'the lost', is a false dichotomy, and the answer is that both are correct. However, the issue I want to look at is: Do we raise our kids with a huge bias towards one set of values or another? To clarify further, I do not advocate the extreme viewpoint that we suddenly expect our kids to know it all, preach, save the world, heal the sick, and make disciples at three years old. However, I feel we have a serious challenge: To make the development of solid 'coming of age' biblical values and beliefs a long-term process beginning in their earlier years, so that the transition of 'coming of age' is smoother.

If we get this right, it won't be a total shock to the system as our children 'come of age', where they have to unlearn all they know, but rather a gradual process of maturing in their faith, and a process that happens in natural synergy with their physiological and sociological development, making it an ongoing spiral approach in a holistic maturation of their spirit, heart, mind and soul. My passion is that we find new methods so that the process for our children's coming of age is gradual and deliberate, well-thought out and well-planned. My desire for the coming generations is that we help them to build biblical values and a good understanding of what it means to be a disciple of Jesus, alongside a personal relationship with the God-head, resulting in a lifestyle that reflects these things; and that we do it early on enough in their journey that their core values and beliefs don't have to be challenged by the very church that gave them the values and beliefs in the first place. Because, in my experience, that's a journey too hard to travel for so many young people, and I believe for us as leaders, prevention is far, far better than cure.

Let's not lose years to reshaping, repairing and rebuilding. Let's use wisdom, strategy, and Godly, biblical inspiration to build great generations. Let's discover our generational vision.

GOD BLESSES GENERA- TIONS

We all hope for a better future. We hope that the *when* will be better than the *now*.

It's right for us as Christians to believe for a better future for our family or churches. However, we cannot just hope, we have to act, because for the *when* to be good, it's important to make wise choices in the *now*. Let me be honest, I had no idea how huge the shift in society has been and how quickly it has happened. I was totally ignorant to and genuinely shocked at the depth and extent of the shift. But it is real, and as I spent more time with the kids in our church, I could not miss the signs of it. It's inescapable and has the potential to be incredibly destructive unless we take action.

The issue of growing up and of generations 'coming of age' and finding their own feet in the faith is not a new one for Christianity. However, I believe it is one that we can approach more effectively. It is an issue we have to keep up to speed with and it starts *now*.

As churches, we've often been slow to catch up with what society is doing and how it's changing. It's obvious in the demographics of most UK churches that we've missed generations, failed to connect with them, failed to keep up, and then had to work extra hard to catch up. That's why I am writing this now. I want to save us those years. Prevention is better than cure, and if we start to act now, we can prevent the potential loss of generations before it's too late. We can prevent emerging adults from feeling isolated and feeling that 'church isn't for me', that 'I tried my best for God and failed' at that point of coming of age.

The primary catalyst for any change is always our own personal change. That's why I am asking so many tough questions in this book, because I have asked them of myself. As the people with the responsibility of shaping these generations, we have to understand the challenges. So let's take an open and honest look. How deliberate is our parenting style or children's church ethos and approach? How different is it to what it was 10 years' ago?

My intention is that you read this with a positive conviction that brings change, not condemnation that causes you to feel paralysed or daunted in any way by guilt or regret, but as a moment of grace and an opportunity to begin afresh from now. Make daily choices from this moment to give this opportunity your dedicated focus and investment

Make time in your diary each week to plan, dream, meet with your partner or team, and start to make changes to how you develop strong biblical values and beliefs into the generations as they come of age. It's not something to feel panicked about or rush into, be wise and do not use fear or control of your children or team out of a place of insecurity, but be discerning, prayerful, receptive to the ideas of others, and do it all in love.

I suggest that as a parent or pastor you think long term and start to plan a strategic flow of how you will help your generation of children 'come of age'. I suggest you make your own study plan to grow your knowledge of the stages of development, especially for your context and environment, as it may well be different to mine. Then also look at biblical teaching and guidance on core values and beliefs. Start to think creatively about how you can build these within your children naturally and organically through who you are, how you are, and what you do as a family or church -- not with rules and regulations like the Pharisees – but by committing to first and foremost modelling what you teach in all you do you. If you model it yourself in line with Matthew 22:39, you are giving them your best – the best you would choose for yourself. It's so important that you personally have experienced what you teach and guide, that you believe it's the best for you, then that which you are giving freely is love – loving your neighbour as yourself. Because only if you truly love yourself, will you have the means to pass the love on for others to access –that's the spread of grace. If you don't model it but teach it and expect it from the children, then it's legalism, which leads to works, not loving relationships. It's crucial we get that one right.

God taught me this in a personal and humbling way. In church, sometimes you know when something is not right – you can see it, and it's physical, but it's also spiritual, right? Well, our kids' musical worship was like that. Nothing bad, but it was lacking in the depth of our heart worship. Kids were too conscious of self and not conscious enough of God. I got my leader head on, prayed, fasted, did all the 'right things'; I felt God speak to me about the kids surrendering. So I talked to the worship team, set it all in place, ready to lead the kids to surrender. I guess somewhere, not even intentionally; it was tinged with the attitude that it was something they needed to do. During this time, our church was hosting a major conference – the sort with international speakers, TV cameras and the like. I was on the front row of seats at the conference, and God just moved in my heart. I felt that although it was already an attitude of my heart, I had to surrender in that moment. It was not a good time, or appropriate, and quite embarrassing, but I felt it was right for me to kneel before God, which isn't popular or done at all as part of the culture in our church. I spent a minute checking with God that he had seen these issues and that this was his timing – or in reality, I was just procrastinating – but eventually I did it wholeheartedly.

The intimacy and love and connection was amazing, it blew me away. It was so powerful and intimate, and I believe this directly correlated with the next thing that happened. A day passed and along came Sunday and kids' church. I was in with the kids and the planned moment arrived for me to lead them in surrender during the worship music, so I went up onto stage at the end of a song. I got on the microphone, ready to speak, and just naturally (without a conscious thought) went to God on my knees again in my spirit and heart, even more so than physically. So without thinking I knelt down, but before I'd even said a word, every kid in the place, seriously, every one, was on their knees. Not just that, they were all in – heart and soul surrendered in amazing worship to God. That was one of the most powerful God-filled moments in kids' church. It was a really sacred moment, full of grace and love, and it changed things.

We have to start now, but we have to start with us.

Let's be honest, developing children and generations is tough, but I think we sometimes fail to see or understand the value of what we do, especially in the long term. Children's ministry is not a department in church famous for glamour or glory. Unlike preaching or leading worship, for example, there's not usually a queue of people waiting to take up the baton. It's hard work and it's often done in the back rooms of church, where you miss out on 'what's really happening'. In my experience, it can be relentless. You can never take your foot off the pedal and it can be an isolated and quite lonely place. Added to this, church doesn't give this ministry a great reputation. Can I be brutally honest? I sometimes think pastors see it as something they don't really know about but want done well so that the church retains families, making it important in that context, but not really a priority for them to directly and personally invest into.

It can be the same story with parenting – sometimes all you can see are the pressures of running a household, keeping on top of the chores, and the pressure to provide and get the bills paid. Our society and pace of living accelerates these pressures, draining us of our energy, causing us to lose our focus of loving and developing our kids.

I recently had the privilege of having a conversation with a key political figure. I was asking for his opinion on the issues in our nation and his answer surprised me. His opinion was that many of our nation's problems could be traced back to a lack in parenting skills, and in particular, a lack of fatherhood. It's not a judgment or a condemnation, but it should charge us as God's family to really support and add value within these huge responsibilities.

I want to be honest enough to raise some of the issues, because if kids' faith is like the story of Cinderella, I don't think Cinderella has gone to the ball yet in Christian culture. I think she is still in the basement doing the dishes and childhood development doesn't yet have the value it requires for us to see the churches we dream of. I don't want you to get me wrong, that hasn't entirely been my family or church experience. I have had strength added by my parents and leaders, strength from which I write this book. But it's important to address these issues, as I know this isn't the case for so many others. We all have a responsibility to support each other, and in order to add value, it first needs to come from within.

Think about your children's and church's future. Not in the abstract of what it could be, but in the reality of what you have now – the younger generations, say up to 30 years old – and what has been invested into them and how that has paid off. You will find both helpful and unhelpful things in the mix, and the good news is that if you are reading this, you're not dead yet, so if you see things you don't like, there's time and grace enough to fix them with God's help.

Consider how you are investing into your current generations. It's easy to be so preoccupied with today and the adult generations you already have, that you miss investing in the adult generations you will have in your tomorrow. To get really practical, it's really simple. The best thing we should be investing in and probably the most important resource we have to add value, is our time—spending time relationally to journey towards a deeper love with people.

Remember: there is no return without investment.

This is an encouragement to be shrewd with your time, and to ensure the family or church you will have in ten years' time is being built today. I'm not advocating you drop everything to focus solely on kids, youth and young adults, but I am suggesting that you start to give it some serious thought, prayer, focus and direct personal investment. Spend time with them, and the people or teams involved. Not by adding pressure by putting a greater demand on you as a parent or leader, but by making a commitment to invest your time in loving them first and foremost. Further than that, if you can, share your help, vision, faith, and finances. All of these investments will not fail to bring you a great return, maybe even the family or church you dream of in a few years from now.

BUILDING WITH WISDOM, UNDERSTANDING & KNOWLEDGE

I deliberately called this chapter 'Building with Wisdom, Understanding & Knowledge', as Proverbs 24:3 got me thinking.

This chapter is not an exegetical Bible study of Proverbs 24:3, so you may have to forgive me if my ideas don't fit the religious 'norm'; this chapter is about an adventure through the creative possibilities for raising up Kids of Jesus, with Proverbs 24:3 as my destination. I will attempt to map out a few ideas on how to get there.

The scripture says: 'By wisdom a house is built, and through understanding it is established; through knowledge its rooms are filled with rare and beautiful treasures.' Proverbs 24:3-4 (NIV)

That was my heart's desire—to build and establish a household and church that is robust for the long term, to see our generations become rare and beautiful. Below is an outline of how I broke this scripture down and used it to guide us in developing a strategy for shaping our children's values and beliefs.

Wisdom: Application of knowledge through good judgment. (Biblical in this context)

Application of God's Word through the Spirit is a solid foundation for all we desire to do. If in the beginning was the Word and the Word was God and with God, then became flesh and dwelt amongst us in Jesus (who sets the ultimate example), then our instruction is in him. After reading this verse and chapter for months as a team, and tying ourselves in knots trying to find out every detail of what God wanted us to do, we came back to the point that God understood the limitations of our human minds and understanding, and that's why in his grace, he gave us Matthew 22:36-41. Phew! We decided to keep it simple in our foundations (but surprisingly complex in application) and base all we did on a love for God and a love for others. Very basic, I know, but try it; it's definitely not as easy as you might think. Now it was from this point that we derived our vision statement to: 'Love God and love others', which was all well and good. You've probably heard and seen it a thousand times before. But we made a commitment that it wouldn't just be a vision statement, but that those two values would be the driving force behind every aspect of reinventing our kids' church holistically so that it wasn't just in a statement of thought, but in the very deeds of all that we do, and in turn, lead our kids to do.

The second point of that scripture is 'understanding' and it's at this point of the scripture that we leave the familiar territory of wisdom. Wisdom is an area I feel that most churches are strong in. Most churches have a strong grasp of what they feel God is calling them to do through his Word and most have a strong, robust vision statement as a result of this. Once we have wisdom as the foundation and our vision statement is established, that is only the start of the process. It is at this point we step out of the aspirational and into our current reality.

Understanding: Grasping mentally to include and encompass

It's sometimes painful to delve into our current reality and it can seem a carnal thing to do, as it's not 'seeing things with the eyes of faith' or the like. Our current reality can definitely frustrate us and sometimes overwhelm us. It can make us feel inadequate and, in its worst cases, strike fear into even the greatest of leaders. But the ability to question, fact-find and understand where we and our families or congregations are at, is a huge strength, and adds so greatly to achieving what God has called us to do.

Let's take the greatest example ever—Jesus. Even Jesus, at the forefront of his miracles, helping people to salvation, still began with understanding. Let's take John 4 and the story of the woman at the well, where Jesus already knew the answers to this woman's issues but still took the time to ask and prompt questions in her to gain understanding, which preceded her salvation. Jesus used the power of understanding to draw people to God and that's what we should do. He wasn't so quick to do the will of God that he didn't bother with understanding where people were at and just steam roll right over them; and at the same time, he wasn't daunted by his understanding of what he was up against; he brought God's kingdom to the situation in front of him. For me, that's the perfect balance.

Here are some things I would say about understanding. Firstly, it's humbling. You realise you don't have all the answers and you need God. That's as healthy a place as any to start. It's humbling being told your best is boring by an eight year old, and finding a ten year old with better ideas than you on how to connect their generation to God. But there is something about that quest to gain understanding that reflects God's heart and draws people to us, makes them feel safe, valued, and included into something greater than themselves.

I would also say that for most leaders, understanding is counter intuitive. We just want to judge things as we see them on face value (without getting involved with the people implicated) and call the shots to fix them, again, without getting too personally involved. However, understanding doesn't really allow for that, because we have to get up close. It's through getting up close that it makes a way for humility, grace and love instead of judgment and legalism. Understanding requires humility and compassion and it fuels a righteous stance against the circumstances, not the people themselves. In my experience, understanding is invaluable in the process of seeing God move. Let me share a few examples. At the start of this whole process, my approach was that as a team, we would take responsibility for our current situation. Again, through Matthew 22:39 and our vision of loving others and treating them as you'd like to be treated, we agreed as a core team that instead of calling the people to serve us, we decided to serve them. That kind of fitted the way I saw Jesus modelling leadership—not to be served but to serve. What was holding us back? Where did we need to make corrections? How did we need to change? These were all questions we asked others about ourselves. We even took the brave steps of asking our team for honest feedback and then the even more daunting (some might say crazy) steps of asking our kids' opinions.

I set about meeting team members and asking what they thought of our kids' work and how they found things, with the aim of understanding how things were from their perspective. To have great kids, we need a great team leading them, so it's vital to understand where they're at and their experience of their role. I wanted to do this face-to-face, even though the team was well over a hundred people, because it gave each person value and invested into them as individuals. I started most conversations informally and with the deliberate intention of putting the team member at ease, joking with them, letting them know they could actually be honest with me about how they felt and what they saw, even if it was perceived to be negative or critical. The wisdom and knowledge that came from the team was amazing. It caught me by surprise. They provided solutions that I would have never considered, resolutions to problems that I would never have discovered! More than that, the bond of togetherness, trusting openness and honesty was refreshing. I also had another purpose to this—to understand them as an individual. I used this time together to get to know my team members; to see them as individuals with different gifts, abilities and passions; to try and help them to find a fit where they could outwork those passions and gifts in the context of kids' church. That was another complete game changer. Just listening is powerful.

The second group I took time to understand was our kids, and we had a lot of them. I observed them and took time to speak with them and ask them questions. I led them to open up about their overall experience of kids' church and with where they were at in life. This was shocking, fascinating, heart-breaking and compelling. If you are a parent or pastor, I would recommend this. I cannot express enough how much I gained from doing this.

I also asked them for advice and suggestions, which I liken to being blasted with a verbal paintball gun. Painful and overwhelming are two words that come to mind; it's only colourful and fun as long as it's not you being shot at! Unfortunately it was me, but it was so useful and insightful, and had a huge impact on what we decided to do.

I would suggest that you prepare your heart and seriously prepare your ego first. But then ask your kids how they find your parenting or ministry; how they would do it in your shoes. It's important to do it in the right context at the right time, to hold the urge to justify yourself or correct them, and just listen. It can be an amazing experience. Be humble and learn.

I realise that the issue of choosing 'either understanding or wisdom!' is another false dichotomy. You need both and you obviously shouldn't let your kids run the show. However, I would just ask: Where does the balance lie between your wisdom and your understanding?

The final part of this scripture is about knowledge, and I think this is one of the greatest untapped resources for us as Christians. We should be discerning but eager to take advantage of the value of other people's education and experience. It's amazing what we can discover from pioneers, not just in the church world but also experts in the 'secular' world.

Knowledge: Information gained through education and experience.

Let me highlight what I think knowledge is useful for. With biblical wisdom as the foundation or the 'what', and understanding as a reference point or the 'where' on the journey, then knowledge can help to show 'how'—'how' to get to the 'what' from 'where' we are. We know from Proverbs 22:6 that we have to teach and train our children, however, the methodology or 'how' we teach can be greatly improved with knowledge. We can use our own education and experience but we can also borrow from the education and experience of others who have invested years into gaining insight into the fields of child development and teaching methodologies. That is what I chose to do, and here's a little insight into how I approached the teaching of children in the Modelling Period (ages 8-11). [1]

Traditionally as churches, we have always taught from the platform, even in kids' church—we teach songs, tell a story, act out a drama etc., all within that teaching style. However, in my experience, even with the most experienced and dynamic communicators, this style of teaching didn't work for all of our kids and it didn't tap into the seven learning styles (the seven learning styles alone are worth your research and should help you a lot). We needed a teaching revolution. I began to seek out knowledge and to research different approaches to teaching, looking for new ways to engage younger generations who communicate totally differently to older generations. After some interesting finds, I came across a few gems, my personal favourite being a teaching style originating in Reggio Emilia, Italy. You can do your own research, but I discovered a teaching process that was fresh and inspiring by following the basic principles set out by Loris

Malaguzzi, and adapting them to work for us. We didn't change the content of what we taught, as that was still the Bible, but we changed how we taught (our methodology), using our own take on the principles of the Reggio Emilia style. [2]

I created a learning process with four steps as follows:

Decide subject: This is where I would have a very direct influence and, taking the children's own interests into account, set the subject about which we would learn— usually a Bible story, passage or scripture. We would present this to the children in a fun and interactive way.

Formulate questions: This is where the kids would get really involved. Having presented the scripture to them, we would break into groups and spark their curiosity. We would get them to look past the scripture at face value and search for what God might be doing, what was happening to those involved, and why. This is directly opposed to the traditional route of discovering this yourself as a leader and sharing your great biblical wisdom and learnt principles with the kids—that's fun for us, but leaves the kids with very little left to explore. This alternative approach helps children to create their own stories and to go on a personal journey of discovery with God with direct revelation, not second-hand information.

Pose hypotheses: Okay, stay with me, as this is where we really get off the beaten track of regular teaching. Firstly, let me define what a hypothesis is: it's a tentative explanation for an observation, phenomenon, or problem that can be tested by further investigation. I know initially that can sound a bit 'unbiblical' but let me assure you that you yourself do this day in and day out, and you are probably so well adjusted to it that you don't even know you are doing it because it's part of your subconscious thinking patterns. To give an example: it's your reasoning for why God let something happen to you, or what God thinks about you. Your answers to these questions are the hypotheses we all form. Even further to this, those hypotheses often shape our faith and beliefs, which in turn affect how we feel and react to God and life. Now let's take a moment to remember that research suggests this area of your brain is developed by the tender age of 10 years old. That's why this approach is so good, because it trains your subconscious to create hypotheses in a healthy way, using biblical values. To get this right, we guide our children to not just make up their hypotheses based on their own feelings, thoughts and assumptions, but to base their hypotheses on God's Word (logos) and to hear the Holy Spirit speaking to them (rhema) through that logos, creating a healthy subconscious pathway, powerful and fundamental for a healthy Christian life. This process achieves even more because we also create a second subconscious pathway, a pathway for checking their hypotheses with their Christian peers and leaders in a natural and organic way, within the safe environment of a biblical critique.

When this is done together with love and openness, this could change everything for our upcoming generations.

Create theories: A theory is a supposition or a system of ideas intended to explain something—a set of principles on which the practice of an activity is based—for example, a theory of education or a theory of music. I hope that as we constantly create theories around the characteristics of God, he becomes someone who our children enjoy spending time with and getting to know. I hope that they are fascinated by finding more ways whereby God loves and guides them, and that they grow personally as part of that process. God then isn't someone we teach about in the abstract, but someone they are developing a relationship with, someone who they look to learn from and become like. Rather than just learning about who God is, we create pathways for walking in relationship with him, learning from him, and allowing him to shape our lives. If we get this pathway right, then the theories will always be secondary and subject to the development of relationship.

I have given the example of this process in the context of church, but wherever possible, I apply it to every area of teaching and learning that I do. You can apply it to parenting or working with your staff teams, etc. It's a method of shared learning and a process that allows everyone to journey with you, and it's amazing, but it doesn't end there. In addition to my research on teaching methods, I also wanted to create a natural and engaging environment where the kids could not only learn things, but also express what they had learnt.

Expression is a vital part of development.

To enable the kids to be able to share and show what God is speaking to them about, creates an amazing opportunity for them to grow in faith and confidence in their journey with God. Again, this led me to further research, as the microphone and the stage just didn't cut it for me as a way for kids to express themselves. So with our teaching methods in mind, I took the complementary approach of studying learning styles. I reasoned that if we could deliver both a successful teaching methodology and an environment for differing learning styles, then that would be a fantastic combination, and after adapting some more information gleaned from studying individual learning styles, I came up with a result that worked for us.

I discovered so many learning style interpretations and applications that I had to narrow them down to what would work for us in our current environment and context. I came up with four creative outlets, which were complementary to our teaching methodology, encompassing all of the different learning styles for our kids.

These were:

Language: Using the art of language to communicate and express, through various means of creative writing or verbal communication.
Play: Both as teams and as individuals, using physically active games and static games/puzzles to express and prove theories.
Arts: Using music, crafts and graphical art to express theories.
Life situations/application: Through conversation and drama role-play, showing how theories can be outworked in everyday life.

These specialist groups would give a structured environment for our kids to express what they had learnt and to express their theories of God within a context that suited their learning style. It gave the kids the choice to be able to express God in a way that suited them, not just to have to conform to a fixed program. Although we could not encompass everything, this offered a great range for our children. Below, I've outlined each stage of the process and what should happen at that particular stage:

Decide subject: Scripture

Formulate questions: The 'why' behind the scripture: Why would God do that? How did it affect the people in the story? How does that affect us?
Pose hypotheses: What could you learn a) About God from that? b) About us from that? Check hypotheses against a biblical framework
Create theories: God did ... because he ... and that means I should ...

Expression:

Language: For this expression, children could write a letter to someone explaining what they have discovered, and, using their theory, explain to the recipient how knowing this about God can affect their lives. Another option time permitting, or if the subject were extended over several weeks, would be to write a short story or poem to express what they had found.

Play: This is a huge area and probably one that we will be least familiar with, but it is possible to devise games, which showcase or add value to a child's theory. For example, a game where a certain response is rewarded, or character is tested against the theory. There are also many drama activities, which could be used to build on the children's theories.

Arts: This expression has limitless options, but to cover a few basics: the children could write songs based on the scripture and their theory of it. They could make (either on paper or via Apps) cartoon stories of their theories, showing how they will apply them in their lives.

Life situations/application: This can be done in such a variety of ways. For example you could run this as a simple discussion group, taking the kids' theories and applying them to relevant areas of their lives. Or, secondly, for the more interactive in the group, this same principle could be acted out in role play, even freeze framing the role play to talk about how their theory could help the situation, then letting the role play continue to see the positive effect of the theory in action.

Pastoral group: The pastoral group is something we schedule every week. Each group has two group pastors who work alternate weeks with the same group. The groups are gender and age appropriate, with up to 8 children in each as best practice. The aim of these groups is to build community and peer-to-peer relationships, with God at the heart of it all. The groups are an opportunity for the kids to come and share their theories with their pastor and peers, and to serve one another in love by applying what they've learnt to each other's life situations and through praying, encouraging each other in the word of God, and by using other spiritual and practical gifts.

To summarise the entire process: we decided to give the children a fixed project to get involved in (based on their theory) within the creative outlets, but always applying it to real life in community. Through this whole process, our aim was that we were not just teaching the children, but helping them to develop their own relationship with God by leading and guiding them in the reading and application of God's Word, and by listening to the still, small voice of the Holy Spirit, helping them grow in wisdom. We taught them that it is natural to share the good things they know about God, that his goodness and love are to be expressed into the world we live in, in a way that is natural to them as individuals. We are no longer teaching our kids from a platform, but building and learning with them, as facilitators of their faith.

[1] **Morris Massey,** https://en.wikipedia.org/wiki/Morris_Massey, *(Accessed on 22/6/15)*
[2] **Loris Malaguzzi,** http://www.reggiochildren.it/identita/loris-malaguzzi/?lang=en, *(Accessed on 22/6/15)*

SPEAK
PRAY
WRITE
DREAM
READ
SHARE
LOVE

UNDER - STANDING GROWTH

Most of the churches we attend are fairly good on Bible teaching. There are many different styles and schools of thought, but on the whole, teaching and understanding the Bible at a basic level is something, in general, we are good at. I think that the greater challenge we face is understanding ourselves, our humanity, the way we tick as humans, the way God created us to form and function and grow in our earthly bodies. There are so many areas to consider such as: how we grow, develop, learn, build our values, build our beliefs, develop our character and become the person we are. These questions have long been the domain of secular scientists, psychologists, and sociologists. Christians can be sceptical when it comes to thoughts from perspectives external to the Bible, as historically, there has often been a battle to defend our faith or a specific theological stance against scientific and academic critique. But let's take that out of the equation for a moment and come at this from a fresh perspective, a perspective that recognises that scientists and psychologists and many others in similar fields have devoted their lives to understanding God's creation in the form of humanity. If we can become a little more open-minded on these subjects, we may realise that some of these great discoveries are fascinating insights into God's creation, and can really serve to help enhance our knowledge and understanding. In my own personal experience, I was shocked at how helpful and insightful external research is and how it can be a real catalyst for teaching our children effectively about God.

Proverbs 23:4 explains how to build a great house, so I'd like to look at the development of knowledge, as this can have a great impact on what we do. So what is knowledge?

Knowledge: Information gained through education and experience.

Education and experience are a great combination. For me, that definition means it's safe to take what we've previously learnt, both through the Bible and through other academic means, and apply it to our experience of God or our current experience (life situation) right now.

The great news is that there is so much helpful information available for us to increase our education and in turn, to help enhance our experience of God. This was a huge comfort and relief to me, as when it comes to understanding how to develop a child, some of the academic information available is unbelievably helpful and offers a great insight into an understanding of God's creation. I have found so called 'secular' research so helpful in understanding growth and development—the when and why of how we become the way are the way we are, and I have become closer to God through it.

Information

There are thousands of books, articles and published documents on childhood development, and the positive thing is that generally, in the broader observations, most information is not fundamentally conflicting and similar trends can be found, though coming from different perspectives. My desire to try and produce something from all of that information that would be quick and easy to both use and understand requires some mass editing. So I have developed a simple table below to give you a basic overview of what I have learnt. It is heavily edited and subsequently from a professional perspective, there are some major 'holes' and bias in the information included. I have deliberately selected information that fits in with my personal context. It's not something I'm overly concerned about providing the information I give is read in that context, and the reader is happy to do their own further fact finding. My personal bias in the information I chose to include, was specifically focused around the social and personal (rather than the educational and physical) development, as I feel this is a more crucial area for us in the context of developing kids of Jesus. In addition to this, I am also really interested in how society and culture are playing their part, so I wanted information that considered and was sympathetic to social trends in the UK. Finally the column entitled 'Ideas for spiritual growth', including the sections 'teaching subjects' and 'pastoral methodology', are entirely my own thoughts based on my research and how it fits with my personal theology.

I simply want to highlight possible methods to you to inspire you to do your own research and to draw your own conclusions. One of the key impacts on development is environment, so I want you to be able draw your own conclusions, which work specifically for you in your environment if mine don't fit your context.

So where did I start? Well within this vast amount of information rather than stick to one single source, I chose to use 3 key pieces of information. Firstly, research commissioned by the UK government Department of Children, Schools and Families and conducted by the University of Oxford entitled: 'Early Years Learning and Development Literature Review.' [1] This review gave a very extensive and broad summary of the information available, and the review had already made edits to include the most useful information, which made it easy for me to 'cherry pick' key information I wanted in the confidence it was from a reputable source. Secondly, to complement this, I also used 'Childhood Development Milestones' from Newport Dyscovery Centre, University of Wales, [2] due to the simplistic nature of the chart. However, thirdly and in complete contrast, I included another section of information, from the opposite end of the spectrum.

This information (although unpublished), I feel, is useful enough and in line enough with published works to give an interesting frame around the main picture of facts. I feel it can help to simply provide a frame of some broader concepts and trends without detracting from the true picture built by the facts. This information is by a popular sociologist, Morris Massey. The resulting information below is a blend of all three, but to follow some form of organisation, I have kept some of the original structure of each.

[1] **Maria Evangelou, Kathy Sylva, Maria Kyriacou, Mary Wild, Georgina Glenny**
Early Years Learning and Development Literature Review
University of Oxford 2009
ISBN 9781847755650

[2] **Childhood Developmental Milestones, Kirby, A. (2012)**
'Childhood Developmental Milestones'. Newport: Dyscovery Centre, University of Wales.

AGE 2

LEARNING ABILITIES	KEY DEVELOPMENTAL AREAS	IDEAS FOR SPIRITUAL GROWTH
Development produced from care givers through their interactions with the child - Sense of self and own identity and value - Emotional warmth - Security - Physical care - Emotional care **Further learning abilities** - Mutually responsive relationships	- Loving relationships - Play - Imitating adult behaviour - Rhymes and songs - Identify with kids - Mutually responsive relationship - Consistent presence - Emotional investment into each individual child - Set an example as a correct response to situations	**Teaching Subjects** - Love - Family - Safety - Trust - Understanding - Fun **Pastoral Methodology** - Modelled and articulated 'on the go' not taught - Initiating interaction - Eye contact - Body language - Example behaviour - Words of encouragement - Questioning - Play - Prayer - Rhymes and songs (e.g proverbs, verses and psalms) - Praying over the children

AGE 3

LEARNING ABILITIES	KEY DEVELOPMENTAL AREAS	IDEAS FOR SPIRITUAL GROWTH
Development produced from care givers through their interactions with the child - Emotional warmth - Security - Consistent presence - Physical care - Emotional care - Emotional investment into each individual child - Mutually responsive relationship **Further learning abilities** - Conversation - Personalised learning - Guided learning - Me and my desires - The desires of others - Pretend play to talk about feelings and intentions of others - Scripts and social narratives - Cooperative conversation and play - Imitating adult behaviour	- Sense of self - Loving relationships - Example behaviour - Play	**Teaching Subjects** - Prayer - We are God's children - God's love for us - Godly identity - Greatest commandment to love - Love others as yourself - Serving one another in love **Pastoral Methodology** - Modelled and articulated 'on the go' not taught - Initiating interaction - Eye contact - Body language - Discussion - Q&A - Role Play - Social narratives - Set an example as a correct response to situations - Identify with kids - Pretend play to talk about feelings and intentions of others

AGE 4

LEARNING ABILITIES	KEY DEVELOPMENTAL AREAS	IDEAS FOR SPIRITUAL GROWTH
Learning abilities - Can recognise rhymes - Asking questions - Can sit and listen for 5mins - Can watch 10mins of TV program - Can sit at a table for 10mins - Can colour in - Can cut and stick - Identify with kids	- Asking questions - Why questions - Development of Trust - Can play taking turns - Development of Shame - Development of Guilt - Emotions - Self regulation of emotions and behaviour - Creativity - Mutually responsive relationships	**Teaching Subjects** - Why God loves us - Being part of God's family - God's unconditional love - Why God chooses us - Salvation by grace - Choosing to follow Jesus - Why we can trust God - Who God is - Names of God - God choices are good choices **Pastoral Methodology** - Praying for each other - Discussion - Q&A - Role Play - Social narratives - Spiritual experiences - Create songs - Craft/Art to express how they see God

AGE 5

LEARNING ABILITIES	KEY DEVELOPMENTAL AREAS	IDEAS FOR SPIRITUAL GROWTH
Engages appropriately in conversation Can form short sentences Can listen to a story for 10mins Describing	- Question and answer - Choosing friendship - Enjoys small groups - Uses imagination to create stories - Can describe	**Teaching Subjects** - Why God loves us - Why God chooses us - Why we can trust God - God choices are good choices - Faith - Jesus' 7 I am's in John **Pastoral Methodology** - Guided prayer: Listening to God and verbalising it - Teaching up front - Conversation one-to-one - Writing ideas - Discussion & Prayer, Peer to peer in groups - Q&A - Role Play - Social narratives - Spiritual experiences - Using faith

AGE 6

LEARNING ABILITIES	KEY DEVELOPMENTAL AREAS	IDEAS FOR SPIRITUAL GROWTH
- Talks fluently - Can learn how to do things through the use of language - Can use language to work thorough scenarios and problems - Can distinguish reality from what is made up - Can read and write to some degree	- Has the ability to see others' perspectives - Gets upset when criticised - Becoming aware of others' feelings - Uses language to work through scenarios and problems - Problem solving through, inquiry, analysis, inference and argument - What, why and how questioning - Can give reasons - Can follow directions	**Teaching Subjects** - God's unconditional love - God's mercy - Forgiveness - Love for others - Choosing to follow Jesus - The great commission - Salt and light **Pastoral Methodology** - Writing about their own God experiences - Reading and writing about biblical God experiences - Use language (question and answer) to work through scenarios and problems - Problem-solving through inquiry, analysis, inference and argument - God is real, give real experiences - What, why and how discovery - Mind maps - Personal application

AGE 7

LEARNING ABILITIES	KEY DEVELOPMENTAL AREAS	IDEAS FOR SPIRITUAL GROWTH
- 20min attention span - Uses serious logical thinking - Starts to understand concepts - Can describe similarities - Increased vocabulary	- Desires to be perfect and is self-critical - Starts to look for independence - Developing reflective thinking - Awareness of own emotions - Worries and may have low self-confidence - Peer pressure and conforming socially - Worries and may have low self confidence - Needs to develop a value of self - Uses blame - Right and wrong - Seeing patterns that connect experiences – e.g. behaviour and what makes me happy? - Highlight apparent disconnections in the above patterns	**Teaching Subjects** - The power of God's truth - Wisdom, knowledge and understanding - The power of the Holy Spirit - Living in God's strength - Sin (separation from God) - God as best friend - Jesus' complete acceptance - Emotions (feelings & failings) - Choice / Will - Placing value on identity not performance - Choosing to follow Jesus for yourself **Pastoral Methodology** - Reading and writing about their own God experiences - Applying what they learn to their own situation - Personal application - Link God and own life - Problem solve using God's ways - Mind maps **

**
- Non-critical discipleship, use questions instead

AGE 8

LEARNING ABILITIES	KEY DEVELOPMENTAL AREAS	IDEAS FOR SPIRITUAL GROWTH
- Can sit and concentrate for 15-20mins - Can converse at almost an adult level - Can read with confidence - Impatient - Need to be loved - Favours group play - Reading may be an interest - Can be sensitive - Can articulate their feelings - Can follow more complex commands - Can be helpful, cheerful and pleasant as well as rude, bossy and selfish	- Seeks to understand the reasons for things - Reading can be a major interest - Conversing becomes a key development tool - Favours group work - Has a strong need for love and understanding - Begins to feel competence in certain skills and may favour certain activities - Emotions change quickly - Developing reasoning - Can keep secrets - More influenced by peer pressure - Has an interest in money - Feelings become more real	**Start discipleship groups** **Teaching Subjects** - Spiritual gifts - Living by the Spirit - Holiness - Know God's love - Why Jesus - Gods word is TRUTH - Being a light to the world - Feelings and failings - Faith - Money / Generosity **Pastoral Methodology** - Self-teaching, e.g. Regio Amlilia Methodology - Reading and writing about their own God experiences - Know God's love - Understanding and listening - Book studies - Use of spiritual gifts - Personal application - Historic inner healing (e.g. Sozo) - Building genuine community - Discipleship peer to peer

AGE 9

LEARNING ABILITIES	KEY DEVELOPMENTAL AREAS	IDEAS FOR SPIRITUAL GROWTH
- Likes to talk and share ideas - Has a best friend - May experience mood swings	- May be critical of self and others - Puts importance on fairness for self and others - Responsible, can be depended upon and trusted - Can write stories - Enjoys to talk and share ideas - May use excuses	**Discovery guides** **Discover God** **Teaching Subjects** - Lamenting - Conviction & condemnation - Generosity - Justice - Grace - Forgiveness - Righteousness - Discipleship - Mission **Pastoral Methodology** - Active faith - Teaching - Justice - Generosity - Peer-to-peer discipleship

AGE 10

LEARNING ABILITIES	KEY DEVELOPMENTAL AREAS	IDEAS FOR SPIRITUAL GROWTH
- Reading to learn - Very capable artistically - Still certain own beliefs are correct - Has a stronger desire to complete tasks - Can keep train of thought even with brief interruptions	- Peer pressure and social conformity become strong influencing factors - Fun and happiness is key - Longer-term tasks can hold interest - Able to memorise and recite - Understands value of parents - May enjoy additional study - Anger becomes a more real emotion - Friendships are important - Critical thinking starting to emerge - Developing conscience and sense of right and wrong - Socialising time is enjoyable	**Discovery Guides for Obedience** **Teaching Subjects** - Love languages - Forgiveness - Communication - Conviction & condemnation - Community - Honouring parents - God strength - Trusting in God - Not living a double life: e.g Daniel **Pastoral Methodology** - Involvement in leadership - Create own projects (e.g. a mission) - Trips and activities - Memorising scripture - Home study - Book studies

AGE 11

LEARNING ABILITIES	KEY DEVELOPMENTAL AREAS	IDEAS FOR SPIRITUAL GROWTH
- Can sit and concentrate for 30mins - Enjoys independent working - Logical arguments - Enjoys mixed disciplines in learning and development (e.g. oral, visual and written)	- Starts to realise others may hold different beliefs - Behaviour at home may be worse than other environments - Story writing skills are strong - Good awareness of right and wrong - May become argumentative - Improving in ability to make decisions	**Discovery Guides for emerging leaders** **Teaching Subjects** - The power of God's truth - Wisdom, knowledge and understanding - The power of the Holy Spirit - Sin - Self - Emotions - Choice / Will - Culture & Faith - History of Christianity (books by John Drane) **Pastoral Methodology** - Reading and writing about their own God experiences - Debating / finding facts (books by John Drane) - Community discipline - Involvement in leadership Create own projects e.g. a mission - Mixed disciplines oral, visual and written

The heart of much of the research I have studied, can also be captured in these brief sections below:

Learning

'The aim of teaching is not to produce learning but to produce the conditions for learning, this is the focal point, the quality of learning.' (Cited in Rinaldi, 2006, p175). [1]

Identity

'Children are born without a sense of self; they establish this through interactions with others (adults, siblings, peers) and within their culture.' (Early Years Learning and Development Literature Review, University of Oxford). [2]

I can't stress how huge a revelation this is. The fact that God's grace is there from the start giving us all an equal start. This shaped my whole approach to kids' ministry, making it one of our primary aims that we should look to build a scriptural truth and God-shaped view of 'self' in our kids, as he really does give us a blank canvas.

Care givers

Children thrive in warm, positive relationships characterised by contingent responses.

Again this is so fundamentally key to how we work with our children. A genuine and sincere proactive love will bring so much positive influence. Even if our teaching methodology is different or even in a worst case scenario poor, this is something we can all get right.

I also thought it would be helpful to include some of the reflected themes of love, which were closely linked to healthy child development.

- Loving, caring
- Identifying with kids
- Listening, reflecting and evaluating
- Recognising, praising
- Placing value
- Mentoring/making disciples
- Adult-guided activities, where children gradually become full partners and finally leaders
- Guided interaction

Children's 'voice'

Conversation is another prime context for the development of children's language and thinking, but also for their emotions. Children are talked at all the time with constant commands, instructions and directions. So for a child to have the opportunity to express themselves, to talk to you, to ask questions, to tell you how they feel and how they see things, is so important for their development on multiple levels.

Teaching

In enhancing children's thinking, it is more important to aim at depth not breadth. Deep understanding is more important than superficial coverage. Repetition is useful along with small, but deep new data sets.

Play

Play is a prime context for development. Examples include:

- - Child lead activities where you can learn about them
- - Pretend, role play—creating 'theories' and appropriate responses
- - Pretend mode to allows children to manipulate actions and events
- - Outdoor play and safe risk-taking

[1-2]   **Maria Evangelou, Kathy Sylva, Maria Kyriacou, Mary Wild, Georgina Glenny**
Early Years Learning and Development Literature Review
University of Oxford 2009
ISBN 9781847755650

Final information source: Morris Massey

Massey suggests that there are 4 major periods that a person will go through in the creation of values and personality. Reading this helped me to group (or frame) a lot of the other information. Below is a brief overview and description of each of the key points of the major periods of development.

Period 1: The Basic Programming Period, which may occur at pre-birth until age 4.
Period 2: The Imprint Period, which occurs from birth until age 7.
Period 3: The Modelling Period, which occurs from ages 8 until 13.
Period 4: The Socialising Period, which occurs from ages 14 to 21.

During our Basic Programming Period, we soak up everything, largely without any filters. What I mean by 'filter' is that at that age, we may not have the ability to determine the difference between useful and 'un-useful' information; it is just information that goes 'straight in', so by age 4, most of our major programming and personality has been formed.

During our Imprint Period, ages 0 to 7, we continue to soak up everything like a sponge; we pick up and store everything that goes on in our environment coming from our parents and other people and events that occur around us. They are all imprinted into us.

The Modelling Period, ages 8 to 13, is when we begin to consciously and unconsciously model basic behaviours of other people. We may also begin to mimic the values of those people.

From Massey's research, he suggests that our major values about life are picked up during the middle of this period, at about age 10. In addition, he suggests that our values are also shaped on where we are and on what is happening in the world at that time.

During the Socialising Period, ages 14 to 21, the young person picks up relationship and social values, most of which will be employed throughout the rest of his or her life. By age 21, the formation of core values is just about complete and will not change unless a 'significant emotional event' occurs (or someone deliberately instigates a significant life-changing event).

With that as a basic overview, we can start to build a picture and gain knowledge around the processes of development that take place as we grow up. If we apply this knowledge to how we parent or how our children's ministries function, we start to understand what environments, experiences, modelling, behaviour, values and beliefs are important to have in our churches and families to help kids develop at each stage of their growth and development.

The only problem with this research is that society is still changing and transforming. Although the stages of development still stand and are recognised, the latest evidence suggests that the ages at which they happen may well be shifting younger and younger, and the evidence of this is showing in our church and probably yours as well.

With this newfound knowledge, it gives us a great opportunity to ask some different questions with a fresh perspective. I suggest you take some time and get into the Bible and look at what you want to build in the different stages of development. Take your time and be thorough. Make sure it lines up with holistic biblical guidance, not just church culture. As a starting point, here are some of the things we have focused on for each of the stages of development.

Kids' Ministry

At each stage, we have chosen some key focuses for our programme and team. They aren't the only things we do, but they command significant focus due to being key development areas.

Basic Programming: Ages 0-4
- Kids program of activities
- Biblical information
- Experience of God
- Healthy environment
- Parental involvement
- Holistic care

Imprint period: Ages 4-7 (some crossover with basic programming)
- Personal connection with God
- Discipleship
- Information and experience of God
- Parental involvement
- Healthy environment
- Holistic care

Modelling Period: Ages 8-11
- Personal journey with God
- Guided discovery about God
- Discipleship from leaders
- Healthy role models
- Environment
- World view

Youth Ministry

Socialisation Period: Ages 11-13 and onwards 13-21
- Personal God
- Discipleship with leaders and peers
- Relationships with peers
- Biblical core personal values
- Biblical social values
- Opportunities to be a part of significant events e.g. Conferences, mission trips etc

START CHILDREN OFF ON THE WAY
THEY SHOULD GO, AND EVEN WHEN THEY ARE OLD
THEY WILL NOT TURN FROM IT.

PROVERBS 22:6 (NIV)

A FRESH
APPROACH

After having my head in scripture and research, and dreaming as a team about all these things we could build, it was always going to be tough to coming back to reality. I was completely overwhelmed by the task ahead of me in kids' church, and daunted by how much it needed to change and how little I had to make that happen. I decided that I needed faith, and the eyes of faith, to see what it could be, but also we needed action in the here and now to do what we could do in the now. So together, with my team, I started from scratch.

But before you read some of our examples, let me help you with your expectations. I would say that if you want to fully change and transition your parenting style or children's church, you need to be willing to commit to a process of change, which will take anywhere from 2-5 years. This is a long-distance, endurance race, not a sprint.

GRACE: LOVE NOT BASED ON PERFORMANCE

TRUTH: GOD'S LOVE DELIVERED IN HIS WISDOM FOR US

It is often really easy to see what doesn't work in your family or church and to get condemned or downbeat about it all. It's really easy to get frustrated with people who don't do things in the way we would like them to (I'm the leader, this is how I want things, so do it), right? But we need to treat first ourselves and then others the way that God treats us, with grace first and truth to follow. Grace is the instigator, the first step where God moves towards us, without an agenda to change us but an absolute commitment to love us and journey relationally with us towards what's best for us. More than that – to help us navigate how to find ourselves through that relationship with Him. Jesus even took the time to understand us, to walk in our shoes as a man, before he helped us. Grace shows us that God doesn't depend on us for taking care of his business – he's way outside and beyond that – but he wants us to be a part of what he's doing on earth; to achieve, be happy, work in harmony with him, to see his Kingdom come and his will be done on earth. We quickly found we needed to get our love in order first and foremost.

This was really helpful to avoid wrapping the team and kids up in condemnation, legalism, or truth without grace, or of making the mistake of applying pressure for them to instantly be all the things we wanted them to be. Granted, our expectations are often for their own good, but unless they are led with love first, they promote works. Our extension of grace was that we agreed that the onus on development would always be on us and not them—that we would do the work to facilitate them to change and grow, and we would do that through our change and growth first. We determined that we would expect nothing of them that we would not model first in our behaviour and also in the structure and program of our children's ministry. We determined that we would give them options, and within those options, we would make God's love and best for them an option that was good enough for them to desire to be a part of it.

Here's what I'm getting at in a practical example. We wanted our kids to be loved. We wanted our kids' team to be there for them, to spend time with them. But our teams were focused on the tasks, on what needed to be done: setting games out, sorting craft, and then talking to the kids after this. It would be really easy as a leader to push the team, to tell them to raise their game, to tell them that they needed to focus. But I knew the teams were giving their best, they were working really hard flat out, and they really did love the kids. So I took the responsibility on us as leaders. I made it my responsibility to model this for the team—to give them the grace of my love, my service and my best, to do for them what I would want them to do for me in that situation. So I prayed and thought and decided that I needed to get off the task myself, to get to loving and pastoring my teams first. I realised I was bowled over with tasks, and my team just reflected that. So I built a bigger team and included people who loved the task side of things, who felt it was their God-given gifting. These people took on some of the admin and task roles in kids' church, which in turn freed me and my teams to pastor – me to pastor them and then in turn for them to be released and empowered to pastor others, which they all loved and did naturally and enjoyed. That's how grace and truth should work in my opinion—us as leaders giving our best, serving in love, and in turn making it possible for others to do the same.

VISION: WHERE YOU WANT TO BE

As you'll know from the previous chapters, we had a great vision as a kids' ministry, we always had. But our main problem was that a vision is abstract and not tangible. It's the effect and not the cause.

I think this is such a key thing that so many of us search for. We know what it should look like. We want to achieve the 'vision', but how to get there, isn't totally clear, and people with you don't 'get it'. That has been a popular sound bite amongst leaders. But the good news is that it's not a great mystery. All we need to do is backtrack a little to discover the cause, because if we get the cause right, then the effect will happen organically and naturally, completely unforced.

The great thing is that the answer is just a case of taking your vision and putting a value on it. All I did was search scripture to see how to love, how the church built it in practice. Then I started to compile a list of things I thought would work for us from that—things I wanted to value, the causes that would fulfil our vision of love; for example, healthy relationships in our community. It sounds a very simple concept, but it often isn't as clear as we think. For example, our vision is to build the church, so we go at it at 100 miles an hour, stressing ourselves and our team out, overloading them with works, until they are so busy with them that they fail to fulfil the vision of loving.

So if the vision is the 'what', then values are the 'how'. In this context, for us, it involved creating totally new approaches to what we were doing and how we did it. I suggest you take your time, think, pray, and search for biblical parallels with your vision to help you create your values. If you are building God's kingdom, then there should be biblical examples in your vision and in the values you're creating. Even if they're not direct examples from scripture, they should be principles you can use to build your values God's way. You search and ask yourself: 'How did people in the Bible create these?'

In a previous example, I mentioned how all of our kids' pastors were preoccupied with the task, not the kids. The team had the vision to love the kids; they had the heart – that was not an issue. But there was still a problem, as the vision just wasn't being fulfilled. I observed for a few weeks and I saw them doing their best to connect with the kids, but they were still too busy, too driven by the task. We had to put values around our vision, to actually value the things we wanted to achieve, to give them time and focus, to make these values what our time and teams were all about. So we completely changed our team roles, and instead of our teams being one-man wonders who had to do it all, talks, snack, games, craft, etc. Instead of this we created Pastoral Groups; from the top down, Team Pastors and Kids' Pastors modelled the process. These were all new roles created as values that forced us to fulfil our vision. We again grew the team and broke down the jobs to people who were gifted in each area, so there were no tasks given to the Team Pastors, just the responsibility to love and disciple the Kids' Pastors.

Again, the Kids' Pastors had no responsibilities other than pastoring a group of around 8 kids. Our core team then worked with them to model values from one leader to another, which in turn got passed down to the kids. Creating this pastoral value enabled the vision to be fulfilled by giving it the total focus of our time and responsibility. The teams were then clear about the vision and clear about what we were valuing, giving them tools to outwork the vision, make connections and build community. They had grasped full-heartedly what it truly means to value and invest in others.

VALUES: WHAT YOU INVEST IN TO ACHIEVE YOUR VISION

We were really excited by these new values. It was like a breath of fresh air into everything we did, it was like the clouds had cleared and we could see a clear way forward. That was until we looked at the practicalities of achieving what we had decided we now needed to do. Then it felt as though all we could see was the huge mountain we had to climb. Standing back and looking at our values in the cold light of day was tough, especially given the resources that we had. Let me be really open and honest with you: at that time, we had around 300 kids a week coming on Sundays. Our team was running at about 2/3 of what it needed to be for our new vision. We had no margin in our budget to employ or outsource or even buy in the resources we needed in order to do things differently. It all added up to what felt like an impossible mountain to climb; it seemed a lifetime's work. But sometimes you have to just start where you are at with what you have. I think Jesus is a great example of this. He had nothing in terms of practical resources, but he achieved everything in terms of seeing God's Kingdom come and will be done.

I think in modern Western society, we can get caught in the trap of the opposite to that, pursuing everything we need and getting little of God. Sometimes the things we feel we need, or believe are essential to our ability to parent or carry out ministry, become huge blockages and barriers. For example, we might believe that without the finances, the team, the building, etc., we cannot achieve what God is asking us to do. When we take this perspective, we often find ourselves in comparison with other families, churches or ministries, and we become blind-sided. I know I've been there, blinkered to the amazing resources right in front of us: our very own fishermen, or a simple pair of sandals, or spit and dirt that heals the blind. The early church's greatest resource was the Holy Spirit, and often I think we don't need much more than that either. I suggest that if you feel overwhelmed and under-resourced, you rest up your frustration and take a bit of time. Relax and look at what you have. Appreciate the great things that God has given you. I did and it filled me with a different type of faith and a fresh excitement.

So, we had volunteers and kids and Sunday. They were our main resources. With these three things in mind, we took these great newly created values and looked at how they could fit together.

For example, with our vision of love and the value of pastoral communities, we looked at our resources. How could we best use our resources within our values to see our vision fulfilled? This started with a real investment into our pastoral groups, and instead of spending time planning with the teams and working on the programme (we built another team to do that), we invested in the pastors—finding out their dreams, passions and gifts, and then investing in them to build those. We also started to add value to them in their own roles, training them how to connect with the kids, talking through the issues the kids were facing. We equipped them to connect with the kids on a social level, giving them skills to draw the kids into conversation, and helping them to connect with each other. This investment into specific training and giving the pastors tools, then spending our time mentoring and building them and the kids, ensured that our resources built towards our vision. We loved our team and added value to them, and they in turn loved and added value to the kids. Everything we did helped grow what we had, and people joined.

RESOURCES: THE THINGS YOU HAVE TO INVEST

Once we had figured out that people were our main resource, and investing into them grew everything, I had to rework everything we did practically within our structure, because our then-current structure really didn't get the best out of our resources (our people). This really ties in with the Vision and Values section as well. With the number of kids and limited resources we had, it would have been easy to just end up chasing our tail, to be busy doing what is urgent, organising, meeting, administrating. All of these things are urgent, pressing you, demanding of you, but the issue with this is that we can get caught in a perpetual cycle of spending all of our time dealing with the urgent and never getting to the important.

When we're stuck in that cycle, we spend most of our time trying to manage our to-do lists, which means we are dealing with the urgent, rather than strategically leading our resources to build towards the important. Finding a healthy relationship between your structure and your resources releases you as a parent or leader to be able to move from managing your resources, to leading your resources. It sounds a very subtle difference, but one will stress you out and demand your time, and the other will empower you to make a change. So we started to use grace, truth and love to structure our vision and values around our resources.

For example: we had a vision of love, and a value of pastoral communities. We had changed the values of our resources in our volunteers, and changed their focus and workload to be in line with our vision. There was still one major piece of the puzzle missing. This was the structure. This covers one of our other major resources—Sundays. I had to ensure that what we did on a Sunday or our 'Structure' of a morning matched our vision and values; not just that our teams were on board with it, but that we used the time we had wisely to also build towards our vision and values. At that time, nearly everything we did was in a large-group format, led from the platform. Our kids were used to being part of a crowd, not a community; and our leaders would connect with them on a haphazard basis. So I got to work on the structure—we changed the entire programme. The first thing we did was create three key times for community within our time structure. Next, we structured the kids into groups. They were all separated into age and gender-appropriate groups of no more than eight. We then put two pastors in charge of each of these groups. The pastors would do alternate weeks but always have the same group of kids, so they would build relationally with them and get to know them, without getting burnt out themselves; they became a tag team. We then structured the morning so that it started and finished with connection time. The first connection time was built around play and social time, and the second was built around sharing and applying what had been learnt; again, building with grace, love and understanding; then truth, wisdom and application. So the structure now also served the vision and values, and all of these things were working in harmony with each other.

STRUCTURE: THE PROCESS THAT BUILDS, SUPPORTS AND PROTECTS YOUR RESOURCES

CULTURE: THE PEOPLE THAT BUILD, SUPPORT AND PROTECT YOUR RESOURCES

Once you are successful in implementing a structure, you will probably feel great. You'll think: 'I've got this sucker down now. This should just work now. Everyone has been informed, has seen the structure, got the vision, got the values', right? However, in most cases, you'll quickly notice that people will just default back to the old habits of thinking and the old way of doing things. But it's fine—that's okay. We don't have to get frustrated and mad at them. It's just human nature. However, it is our responsibility now as leaders to work with our teams and (as long as they are in agreement with us) help them to 'get' or 'become' the culture.

Culture is most effectively spread through relationship, and for change to really work, we as leaders have to be close with the people we wish to catch it. The closer we are, the quicker the culture will spread. The spread of culture is the responsibility of the leader. We have to pull our people close and love them first, desire the best for them, and give them our best. Don't force them to go with the flow of the culture, but find ways that they can flourish in the vision, values and structure you have created—ways that suit them—and inspire them to live up to it.

Love, grace and truth, vision and values, values and resources, resources and structure.

You just have to commit to revisiting this whole process over and again with your team. I found that they defaulted very quickly back to the way things were, to how they'd always done things. I had to repeat the same process as above, but for each individual role, not just for the organisation as a whole. This included a process of reinvesting into the change of each of the key members of my team, and creating new pathways of thinking and working practices for each of them. I also ensured that what I did was scalable and easy to replicate so that they could do the same for others who they were pastorally responsible for. I committed personally to setting the standard, loving, and mentoring my team; to training them in the how and helping them to discover new.

INVESTING FOR A

RETURN

This is an investment for a return—a long-term, consistent investment, with a great long-term, generational return. If you're still not convinced, think about this on the flip side. Take a moment to consider: If we don't put in the hard work now, how much work will it be in the future trying to help people with unbiblical values, or unbiblical theories; or, to be practical, bad attitudes, or an aversion to taking responsibility for their own faith; or even worse, someone who feels church doesn't love them or isn't for them, that they don't fit in, like no one was there for them? These things can take decades or longer to undo, and we don't always get the chance to undo the damage in full, or even at all.

I'm not saying that if you invest in kids and in ways I've suggested over the long term you'll never face these issues or challenges, or that you will have a perfect family or church, but I do think we'll have more of a fighting chance at building wholesome, robust and healthy generations who are better prepared to 'come of age' and to live the rest of their years equipped and empowered, if we put real heartfelt study into who God taught us to be and how he instructed us to live.

As a long-term investment, this is a shrewd thing to do. It means we are committing to building our future. It also means that it is a long-term, consistent and continual investment, so there's no need to panic and try sort everything out in the next six months. Instead, we can just commit to taking our time, giving this some incubation space with people around us who we can trust. We can act now; but act out of faith and love, not out of fear or reaction.

Let me share some ideas of what to invest into.

Coming of age
I would suggest that one of the most important, wise, strategic investments we can make, is to work with those involved in developing the kids, youth and young adults in our churches, families or communities. We must work with them to develop a strategy for helping generations to 'come of age' in, as far as is possible, a succinct process. For us as families and church leaders, we need to take the time to use wisdom, understanding and knowledge; to implement love, grace, truth, vision, values, resources, structure and culture to create a smooth process for coming of age. Let's also agree to future-proof this process with a common understanding that this isn't a one-shot deal. Society and culture will change, along with our resources and environment, and we need to have a constant commitment to assessing all we do and to tailoring it to work in the current times and generation.

79

Family

Once children have come of age, if we have a robust strategy in place for it, then they should already be active Christians and well-established. But why leave our strategy there? Let's plan ahead and be deliberate in preparing these generations for the next life stages. Let's support these generations in their social groups to be prepared for finding and choosing husbands and wives, with biblical guidance, values and criteria, rather than just many cultural ones of external beauty, chemistry and social status. Why stop there? Why not prepare them then for family? Let's have one generation working with another to pass on their wisdom, understanding and experience; especially when it comes to the big things of dating, marriage, family life and children, money, career and crisis. Let's help our generations to be prepared. Let's facilitate older generations to share their wisdom and leave a legacy. Let's engage with all generations and life stages to share wise, biblical frameworks to build solid, biblical beliefs and values before they even have to make the practical choices, so they're on the front foot and ready to make the best of life.

Can you invest when you are poor? If this all sounds a bit full-on, a bit overwhelming, that's not a bad thing. I was personally bankrupt for knowledge and power to do what I felt was important, but I saw God really turn up. The best thing about that, is in bankruptcy or self-lack, there was plenty of room for God. Plenty of room for him to turn up and do HIS thing. All that was needed of me was plenty of desire on my part to ask and seek a way for that.

I just want to share a story of one of our children, a kid who hasn't always thrived with traditional kids' church as it was. I loved this kid, did my best to connect with him and help him connect with God, but there was no 'feel good' moment where I thought 'he's got it.' So I just carried on being 'ineffective' but prayed, did my best, and dedicated him to God. He has come alive in a way that I could take no credit for – it's the Holy Spirit. This kid is quite an unassuming 7-year-old boy and I want to share a story his mum recently shared with me, just from his everyday life.

The family had been out for a meal in the local city centre. It had gotten quite late so the dad had taken the youngest child to collect the car and meet the mother and son outside the restaurant. The mother and son went outside, where they were confronted by two drunk men having an altercation. The mother thought, "How can we avoid this?" in order to protect her child, but the boy spoke and said, "Mummy, we need to sort this!" So his mum very reluctantly tried to intervene verbally, to no effect. At this point, the son looked up at his mum and said, "Mum, it isn't working, let me sort it." He stepped over to the first man and took hold of his forearm. The man instantly stopped and turned to look at the child and said, "I'm sorry, son." At that point, the child took the other man's forearm. He also froze and apologised just as quickly. The child completely stopped both men in their tracks and the fight was over. The child said nothing to them, just stepped back to his mum and said, "There you go, mum, all you had to do was pray for them."

This stuff excites me; it's so far outside and beyond my expectations, and if it's cultivated at this age, can you imagine the impact of a life lived like that, day in day out, over the next 80 years? That's what it's about. Neither my team nor myself can take any credit for any of the fruit in this child's life. We haven't told the children to do any of this stuff or even advised them that this is what they should do, as you can imagine! It's just the natural fruits of a life cultivated with the Holy Spirit. The credit, praise and glory belongs to God because of the work he is doing in his heart. I'm just glad I was bankrupt enough to make space and time within kids' church to allow the investment of the Holy Spirit to grow.

The aim of this book is not to give all the answers, as our kids' church is reassuringly not perfect by any means. Your journey will not be identical to ours. However, what I have experienced is just too compelling to not raise the questions and share some of the thinking, which I pray, hope and believe could make it easier for you to make your own journey. Let's not worry about what is passed, or condemn ourselves for what we didn't know or see. Let's agree to diligently invest from right now into the amazing family of God and the church we believe God for.

Let us use wisdom, knowledge and understanding to equip the family of God and the church of all ages with equal focus, care, concern, love and investment. Let's be wise builders of God's kingdom. Most excitingly, it gives you the chance to build the family or church you always dreamed of both now and to come.

CHILDREN ARE AT THE
VERY CENTRE OF LIFE
IN THE KINGDOM OF GOD

MARK 10:13 (MSG)

CONCLUSION

In reading this book, you might think we have the greatest kids' ministry in the country, right? That's not the case. I'm fairly new at it and although I have a lot of ideas and inspiration, this is about a journey, not a destination.

Most people over estimate what they can achieve in a year, but under estimate or fail to look at what they can achieve in 10 years.

It's great to take a step back and be deliberate and strategic, but it takes time to implement. However, there are things we can enjoy on the journey now, and my aim as a kids' pastor is that our kids experience first-hand the love of God and the ways to connect relationally with him. Nothing can compare or compete with a personal experience of God, where his eternal truths become our personal truths. For me, much of this book and my desire can be summed up in this statement:

We don't just give kids information, we facilitate revelation.

One of the greatest opportunities in parenting and pastoring, after loving, is to engage kids in spiritually stretching activities. This has been a real eye opener for me, when we have offered opportunities to the kids to experience things that we feel are for 'adult Christians', or the 'spiritually mature'. It's amazing how kids can just engage with God in ways you just wouldn't think possible. For me, it's summed up in Luke 18:16 'The Kingdom of God belongs to these'.

I think kids lack the inhibitions, baggage, doubt or lack of trust that so many of us struggle with. They often just simply hear and do. Which sums up Matthew 18:3 and the child-like faith. The trait I have seen that they do struggle with is consistency in this faith. However that's no great worry at this age and that's why we are here to guide, pastor and most of all love them.

Every step is closer
Raising kids as a parent or pastor is a deep-water experience, and ultimately, every child is unique and individual. This is why there is no single defining path, and such a broad spectrum of truths around kids' development. Within these truths I've only been able to encompass a small amount of information. However, the closest thing research points towards as a universal truth, is love, which is unsurprisingly also the greatest commandment. Love is the one thing that EVERY child needs and through the highs and lows that inevitably come, no matter how many mistakes we make, remember that love never fails.

Unsurprisingly, the research supports Jesus' summary on human kind's interaction in Matthew 22:39—that the greatest thing we can do for humanity is to love each other.

The research showed that emotional investment is the greatest deliberate 'teaching' we can do. I say 'teaching', as this is really a heart condition for us and a heart connection with kids. With love as the foundation, no matter what we do in raising our kids, everything will be a step closer to what is best for them. That's why this fits so well with Jesus' summary of the law and commandments. Everything we need to do is encapsulated in loving. This gives us peace in our approach, as the strategies and ideas I have written about are secondary to the love they should facilitate. **Love never fails.**

The power of our personal commitment to love is not to be underestimated. In their review of literature, David et al concluded: 'A key factor enabling children to overcome adversity and challenging life situations was the presence of at least one 'very nurturing relationship'.

My conclusion is to echo Jesus and ask you to love one another, to be at least that ONE.

Be blessed.

Big Love, Pete.

THANK YOU

———————————————

I'll finish with a great thank you. If you've taken the time to read this, if you are investing in children's lives as a parent, professional or a pastor, thank you. My prayer, as you read this, is that you will experience more of his love; that you would be able to pour that out over the kids in your world, thereby reflecting that father heart of a loving God.

A few personal thanks. As in everything I've done, I've stood on the shoulders of giants. There are so many great people I've read, researched, and learnt from, and others I've talked with, so to name a few:

Firstly, my family—my wife Erin for being God's gift to me in every way I need. My Dad and Mum for raising me to question everything, to love learning and to always search for more, but in it all to be a more loving, humble, genuine follower of Jesus. My bro & sis for keeping me real, and humble, and for teaching me more about life than they'll ever realise.

My church—Steve and Charlotte Gambill for their heart, and Steve for his prophecy that kick-started this thinking. My kids' church kids for teaching me everything I never knew; and my kids' pastors for their amazing passion, heart, gifts and commitment. Also to Colin Bloom for being who God has called him to be, which is enough in itself. But most specifically for asking me the most unavoidable, daunting and inspiring rhetorical (but not really) question. The funny thing is I bet he won't even remember it – just another normal day.

And the final say on everything, thank you to God for your love, grace, mercy and truth. Any good I ever do comes from you. Thank you.

CONTACT

IF KIDS OF JESUS HAS SPARKED
CURIOSITY, CREATIVITY OR QUESTIONS
AND YOU WOULD LIKE TO CONNECT WITH
US, WE WOULD LOVE TO HEAR FROM
YOU.   KIDS@LIFECHURCHHOME.COM

KIDS OF JESUS TAKES A FRESH PERSPECTIVE ON HOW WE RAISE OUR KIDS AND APPROACH KIDS' MINISTRY. IT IS DESIGNED AS A RESOURCE FOR PASTORS AND PARENTS ALIKE. KIDS OF JESUS LOOKS AT SOCIETY TRENDS, CHURCH CULTURE, RESEARCH AND CHILD DEVELOPMENT, TO GIVE A WELL-ROUNDED AND ROBUST RANGE OF CREATIVE WAYS TO RAISE KIDS OF JESUS IN THE CONTEXT OF TODAY'S WORLD.

IF YOU ARE RAISING KIDS PERSONALLY OR PROFESSIONALLY, TIME IS A PARAMOUNT. KIDS OF JESUS HAS BEEN DELIBERATELY COMPILED TO BE READ IN UNDER 4 HOURS, WHILST MAINTAINING INTEGRITY OF CONTENT BY OFFERING MANY CREATIVE AVENUES FOR FURTHER RESEARCH AND APPLICATION, WHICH YOU CAN CHOOSE TO TAKE AS FAR AS YOU WISH.

KIDS OF JESUS IS WRITTEN BY PETE GARDNER, KIDS PASTOR AT LIFE CHURCH, BRADFORD, AND SHARES CREATIVE SOLUTIONS TO HIS OWN PERSONAL ADVENTURE OF RAISING KIDS OF JESUS IN MINISTRY.

Printed in Great Britain
by Amazon.co.uk, Ltd.,
Marston Gate.